Under the Table
and Screaming

Under the Table and
SCREAMING

VOLUME 1
Twisted Branch
Tea Bazaar

Erin O'Hare
Edited by Jay Mackenzie Baker

WTJU 91.1 FM

Charlottesville, Virginia

Photo by Angel Olsen

All rights reserved.
Published in Charlottesville, VA by WTJU Radio,
a department of the University of Virginia.
wtju.net

This work received the support of the UVA Arts Council, the UVA Vice Provost
for the Arts, and Virginia Humanities.

LIBRARY OF CONGRESS CONTROL NUMBER: 2023907837

ISBN 979-8-9880587-0-0

eBook ISBN 979-8-9880587-1-7

Cover artwork by Thomas Dean.
All portraits by Sarah Everton.

We acknowledge the Monacan and Manahoac people, the traditional custodians of the unceded land of Charlottesville, where the events in this series take place and where this series was researched, reported, and written.

The title of this series is a reference to the Dave Matthews Band's debut full-length, *Under the Table and Dreaming*. A million and one pepperoni pizza slices worth of thanks to Alan Goffinski for coming up with it, and to everyone who laughed at it when WTJU General Manager Nathan Moore presented the options.

Contents

Note from WTJU

WTJU is more than just a radio station. I mean, it *is* a great radio station, serving UVA and the surrounding communities for nearly seven decades with classical, jazz, rock, folk, blues, world, r&b, hip-hop, and more. All hosted by your friends and neighbors who share your passion for music that moves you.

In Charlottesville's vibrant music ecosystem, WTJU is the fertile soil that nourishes. We bring people together through music and conversation, feeding a community that is curious, connected, and inclusive. Where there is music in Charlottesville, WTJU touches it.

What *does* it take to nourish a vibrant, independent music scene? It requires people who are passionate and committed. It requires people to run venues, bring people together, and create new sounds. In this zine series, you'll meet some of them. And just like we do on-air, WTJU will amplify their voices and enrich our culture. I'm so glad we can, and I'm glad you're along for the ride.

— Nathan Moore, WTJU General Manager

Why Under the Table?
Why Screaming?

Dave Matthews Band is by far the most famous musical act to emerge from Charlottesville (so far). Some folks cherish the local ties to DMB, whose titular frontman got his start as a bartender at Miller's downtown. Others are constantly trying to get out of the shadow the band casts in American popular music history.

Under the Table and Screaming gives a nod to that long shadow cast in the 1990s while delving into the people, places, and stories that keep our vibrant local music scene alive and thriving today. Because, despite DMB's success, they're not a quintessential Charlottesville band; there is no quintessential Charlottesville band, or even bands. There is no "Charlottesville sound." There are, in fact, a lot of sounds made in Charlottesville.

The music scene here isn't just dudes playing indie rock and jam bands for college kids (even if some of those jam bands really rock): It's the jazz legend who taught John Coltrane and Yusef Lateef and later lived, rather quietly, in Charlottesville. It's the female hardcore punk vocalist singing about feminism and identity in both English and Spanish. It's the teenager writing raps in his bedroom. It's the folk guitarist who's traveled the world.

Charlottesville's music culture is rich and varied, but discovering it takes some intentional effort. And the variety isn't necessarily what's touted by the venues that are part of the capital-M capital-B Music Business, which, in Charlottesville, mostly takes the form of Red Light Management, founded and owned by former DMB manager Coran Capshaw. The variety is instead found in restaurants and bars, in tea houses serving vegetarian food, in a house behind a massive magnolia tree. It's in the auditorium of an African American heritage center. It's in bedrooms and basements and backyards.

Some genres and artists have had to struggle for space more than others. And it's not easy. It takes decades of effort and an endless amount of heart. The work is always ongoing.

But if a town wants a local music scene, it must make the space for it. It must nourish it.

This series is about the ever-evolving group of people and places who've done that needful work, creating and keeping the flame of an independent local music culture. It's about those who have championed music made by and for the people who live here. And it's about the many ways to keep that music alive: start a band, bring your friend's band to town, set up a show, make posters, write about local acts, pay for a ticket, or buy some merch. Go to a show and maybe even dance around a little.

Under the Table and Screaming is about a local music scene. Every place has one, and this one is ours.

Under the Table

and Screaming

TEA BAZAAR

Twisted Branch Tea Bazaar is a long and narrow room on the entire second floor of a rowhouse-style building on Charlottesville's pedestrian mall. By all accounts, its décor and vibes haven't changed much since it opened in 2002. Its bones are mostly dark wood, and the walls are painted warm, earthy colors. The kitchen and register are right out there in the open, separated from seating with a long, tall counter. A variety of lamps in a myriad of colors hang from the ceiling, and seating options abound: couches and cozy armchairs, curtained booths, deep benches covered in pillows, proper tables and chairs up front, or even floor cushions and low tables on the raised stage, near the windows overlooking the Downtown Mall. Carvings, elaborately framed mirrors, and artwork cover most of the wall space, as well as a shelf full of tea pots and cups for sale. A few well-worn rugs strewn throughout absorb some of the restaurant din, along with some draped fabric. There's a back patio, too, where folks can go to eat their food, sip their tea, or smoke hookah.

"No other venue that I've played in my life has a signature scent," says percussionist Steve Snider, who's played everything from rock to experimental jazz in the space. "Other people can talk about how CBGB's smelled, or whatever. I know how Tea Bazaar smells, and I will never forget. It smells like the happiest hippy in the world having the worst day of their life."

"It's a very cozy and extremely fragrant restaurant," says Dave Gibson, who's played and seen dozens of shows at the tea house. "You always have to really plan out your outfit for the show. You don't want to need to wear any of it again for at least a couple of days, 'cause it's gonna smell like Tea Bazaar for at least a week."

"Stinky but fine," says Renee Reighart, who, like her husband, Gibson, has both played and seen many shows at Tea Bazaar.

"If you run into a friend who just left the Tea Bazaar, you ask them, 'Oh, were you just at the Tea Bazaar?'" says multi-instrumentalist and singer Gina Sobel. "It's such a pervasive odor that's not unpleasant, but is very distinctive."

"It smells good," says Tyler Magill.

Get Twisted

The Musical History of Twisted Branch Tea Bazaar

When touring bands arrive at the Twisted Branch Tea Bazaar they quickly learn what local bands have known for more than 20 years: it's the worst load-in on the East Coast, probably the worst in the continental United States.

A sandwich board standing on Charlottesville's Downtown Mall promises warm tea, chai milkshakes, vegetarian food, and hookah on the second floor of the brick rowhouse-style building above. But Tea Bazaar, affectionately known as "the tea house," is accessible only by a few tall flights of jag-

ged stairs with half-walls and metal handrails. A band's worst nightmare, made worse by the fact that they can only schlep their heavy amps and instruments up all those stairs *after* lugging it all to the door—Tea Bazaar's location on the pedestrian mall means there's virtually no nearby parking. Bands in the know idle their vans on the closest cross street, unloading their gear while one person stands with the dwindling pile of equipment as other members carry it up those famously precarious stairs.

It takes forever. It's sweaty, especially in summer. It's exhausting. Sometimes it's downright dangerous. Longtime local experimental and occasional rock musician Tyler Magill once fell down the stairs carrying an amp and, in the few seconds he was airborne, thought he might sail through the plate glass window opposite the stairs and land in a heap on the Downtown Mall, before landing on his knees.

But oh, is it worth it.

Matteus Frankovich, founder of Twisted Branch Tea Bazaar. His first employee, Jason Andrews, booked the first Tea Bazaar shows.

Matteus Frankovich opened the Twisted Branch Tea Bazaar at 414 East Main Street in 2002. After steeping in tea culture while living in Portland, Oregon, he traveled to China, Japan, India, Morocco, Egypt, and elsewhere, learning about the world's diverse tea traditions and rituals before deciding to move back to the East Coast and, as he puts it, become a "tea-evangelist."

He chose Charlottesville because it was close to family and full of creative people. But he needed a righthand man, preferably someone with carpentry skills.

Thankfully, Jason Andrews, Frankovich's college roommate's best friend, had those skills and the desire to move. Andrews ditched Richmond for Charlottesville and helped Frankovich build out the tea house. Known as "The Dooch" (a nickname his mother gave him) to his pals, Andrews had been involved in the Richmond music scene, and he and Frankovich built a small stage into the tea house to host shows when they wanted to.

"My vision was tea and the ambiance of all these places I had visited," Frankovich says. "The energy [behind it] was to create a public living room and open it up to folks and whatever energy they brought in there that kind of resonated. The original intent was that music was going to be a small part of this tea house idea. It was almost an aside, an afterthought. When we were designing the place, you'll see that the stage isn't really that big, probably one of the smallest stages in town.[†] But that hasn't inhibited the grandeur of the shows that've played there over the years."

> Atlanta-based group Dark Meat, with up to 17 members, probably holds the record for most people on the tiny stage.

Tea Bazaar quickly earned a reputation for its hospitality toward bands, who got a meal and a couple free drinks per band member, plus a hefty cut of the door. Frankovich lived in the apartment above the restaurant, and he and Andrews often stayed late to hang out and party with the bands, who slept overnight in the tea house before piling in their van and continuing on to their next tour stop.

At least once, Frankovich let people know Tea Bazaar would be closing for the night by yelling, "if you're not staying for the orgy, please leave now!"

"It was kind of an anarchic place" in its early days, recalls Tyler Magill, a longtime local WTJU DJ and experimental and electronic musician. "For a very brief period, it became a Tokyo Rose[†] kind of venue, except a little more so." Frankovich was known to jump from table to table during late-late-night post-show band hangs, something that didn't really fly in Tokyo Rose, a venue located in the basement of a legit sushi restaurant.

TOKYO ROSE – Former home for Charlottesville punk, hardcore, and rock music. More on page 57.

"Frankie and Dooch were interested in having a certain sort of scene, a certain sort of celebration, in a sense, what people started calling the 'temporary autonomous zone,'" says Magill. "I think they really wanted to make a place where people felt free."

Musically, it was a place where local rock and rock-adjacent artists who "thought a little harder about the music" could do just that. In a lot of ways, those bands were carrying on a tradition started by local punk/noise duo The Happy Flowers[†] in the mid-1980s, says Magill.

Tea Bazaar showed up just in time. A year after it opened, in 2003, the Pudhouse, a practice space-slash-residence on Goodman Street in Belmont that also operated as a DIY venue, shut

THE HAPPY FLOWERS – A noise punk duo formed by John Beers (aka Mr. Horribly Charred Infant) and Charlie Kramer (aka Mr. Anus) sometime around 1983. The band got started not long after Beers and Kramer founded The Landlords, one of Charlottesville's first punk bands that played shows at one of the only spots in town that supported that music: Muldowney's, a lesbian bar. Both Beers and Kramer were UVA undergrads and involved with WTJU at the time. Their song "Mom, I Gave The Cat Some Acid" was an underground hit. The band went on to release a couple albums via Homestead Records while touring up and down the East Coast.

down.* Tokyo Rose stopped having music the following year, in 2004. The tea house was there to carry those scenes along.

Magill, a Pudhouse and Tokyo Rose regular, debuted his rock band, Bucks and Gallants, at Tea Bazaar's one-year anniversary party. Magill remembers wearing "a fuckin' biking unitard" and going barefoot for the set. It's a good thing, too, he says, because someone in the audience heckled him, and he remembers shouting something to the effect of, "You are so lucky I am not wearing shoes, because I would kick you in the balls so hard right now."

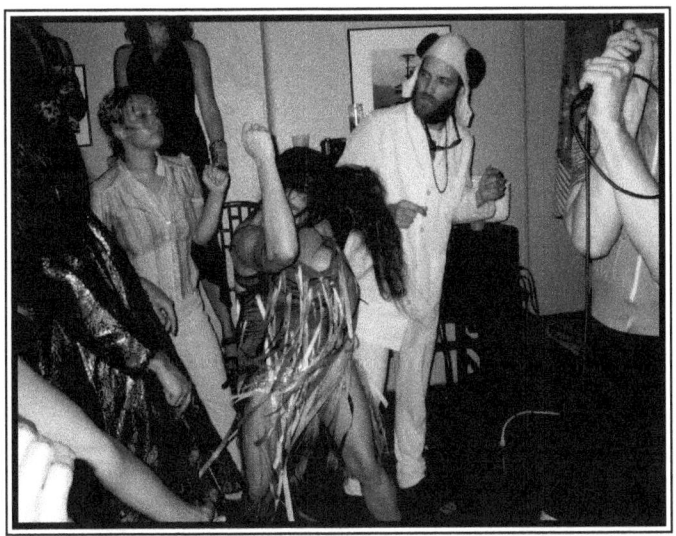

Cathy Monnes (center) dances to a Bucks and Gallants set during the Tea Bazaar's one-year anniversary party in 2003. Photo by Danny Shea.

Bucks and Gallants opened for The Rah Bras, a Richmond band who played raw pop-pomp-punk on synthesizers. The Rah Bras' drummer walked across the tables singing "Pony" at one point.

"That show was great," says Magill. "There's others I really can't remember, but there were some amazing shows."

"We were very excited to have a place that was interested in getting that kind of music," says Magill of Tea Bazaar. "You had all the people in town who were here for Tokyo, like, it was kind of our last gasp—we were all in our early thirties, mid-thirties, starting to actually realize the consequences of the lives we had led," he says, laughing. People would show up to Tea

---

* More on the Pudhouse coming in a future issue.

Bazaar and party hard, and "it's always been great, no matter who ran it," he adds, noting that after Frankovich moved out of the upstairs apartment, he sold the spot to longtime employee Gwendolyn Hall. While the slumber parties faded, Hall and a revolving list of younger folks took over the booking, keeping the spirit of the venue alive.

(Above) Tyler Magill gets out in the crowd during the Bucks and Gallants set.

(Below) Richmond band the Rah Brahs play Tea Bazaar's one-year anniversary party in 2003.

(Left) Tyler Magill, longtime Charlottesville musician who has played in Bucks and Gallants, Grand Banks, One Hundred Dollars, Gallaga, Mss., and who performs solo as Carry. He's been a WTJU DJ for more than 20 years, currently hosting "The Broadcasting System."

Tea Bazaar has hosted an eclectic selection of music from the get-go, and like any venue, the show calendar depends on the tastes and approach of who's booking.

Oftentimes, Tea Bazaar bookers have had the foresight to bring in (usually indie rock) bands that played bigger venues like The Southern Café & Music Hall, or even The Jefferson Theater, the next time they'd pass through town. This was the case with songwriters like Angel Olsen and bands like Speedy Ortiz, War on Drugs, Kurt Vile, Future Islands, tUnE-yArDs, Gogol Bordello, Washed Out, Future Islands, and others. And Gillian Welch played there even after she got famous.[†]

Angel Olsen took this photo of the audience that gathered for her show at the Tea Bazaar in October 2012. Olsen is signed to the Jagjaguwar label, which was founded in Charlottesville. Photo by Angel Olsen.

It's been important to the growth and development of local groups and artists, too. For a lot of folks, it's an honor to play the room, given all it's done for the local scene, and for some, playing Tea Bazaar is the first time they'd played music outside of their basements and bedrooms.

And, because of the open-mindedness of Tea Bazaar and the people who've booked it, it has welcomed everything from avant-garde jazz to electronic music, from local folk to hip-hop and raucous indie rock. They've also held poetry readings, haiku slams, and country Christmas concerts complete with homemade cookies.

That open-mindedness, and the perception of Tea Bazaar as a "cool" or "hip" place can feel exclusive to audiences, and even to artists.

"They've always prioritized more underground, or avant-garde, or experimental stuff, not just genre-wise, but lifestyle and aesthetic-wise also. I appreciate that," says Devon Sproule.[†]

"I think I felt, and was, not cool enough to play there," Sproule says. That is, until she started playing with New Boss, a local rock band with its own genre that it calls "twee boogie."

THAT GILLIAN WELCH SHOW -
Welch had a night off from touring and her pals in Old Crow Medicine Show rang up the tea house to ask if it could accommodate her for a last-minute set. This was pre-social media, but word still spread quickly. Within a couple hours, the room was packed all the way to the back and in a rare moment of quiet (Charlottesville audiences are notoriously chatty) people were totally silent so that everyone could hear her play.

"It was amazing, and a testament to Tea Bazaar's ... 'practice what you preach' sort of thing,' " says Sproule. "Like, people want to play there because they know that the people who are going to hear about it aren't going to be annoying, you know?"

Devon Sproule, avant-garde folk songwriter.

DEVON SPROULE -
A songwriter and singer who grew up at Twin Oaks community in Louisa County and has been playing her singular vision of folk music on local stages since she was a teenager. All of Sproule's albums have received critical acclaim, and her music reaches audiences far outside of Virginia. In 2012, she and her husband (and frequent collaborator) Paul Curreri performed Sproule's original song "Old Virginia Block" on legendary UK music television program Jools Holland Live. In 2014, The New Yorker published an article instructing its reader with its title: "Listen to Devon Sproule."

"It wasn't really … it wasn't coolness, either. It was a style of music. Maybe it was the scene, or maybe I was projecting. But I always sort of half understood and half felt like 'oh darn, I wish I could play there.' Once I started letting go of my *need* to play there, I started getting invited more," Sproule says, laughing.

Jeyon Falsini, who's likely booked and managed more venues than anyone else in Charlottesville (including the tea house and the very musically and culturally diverse Annex/Ante Room)[†] calls Tea Bazaar "Booking Agent 101." The person who books the shows also runs the shows, from striking tables and chairs to setting up the PA and the mixer.

> **THE ANTE ROOM –**
>
> The Ante Room operated, and overlapped with Tea Bazaar, from 2012 to 2018. It was originally called The Annex before being re-named. At the west end of the Downtown Mall, facing Water Street, it shared a roof with an ice arena and a gay bar/restaurant, Escafé. The building holding all three spots—and the cultures they supported—was demolished to build the CODE building, a co-working and think tank space.

That person also runs sound and runs the door—that part always includes getting the cover charge out of people claiming they just want to smoke hookah and therefore shouldn't have to pay, and sometimes involves dealing with people who want their money back if they don't like the music. That person is also charged with assuring bands unfamiliar with the space that yes, this load-in will be worth it … they hope.

Then there's promoting the shows—making and posting flyers, etc.—and trying to get enough local folks to come out, but not so many that they reach capacity and have to turn people away. Annie Dunckel, who booked Tea Bazaar in the mid-2010s, says that one thing that can be frustrating about booking shows in Charlottesville is that the scene is cliquey, so, if one of the cliques' bands weren't on the bill, people wouldn't really show up. "But that's the art of booking," she says. Sometimes you have to bring in the popular local bands to get people in for the touring bands or book

Annie Dunckel booked Tea Bazaar for a few years and also lived and booked at Magnolia House, another Charlottesville DIY spot.

a popular touring band to get people in the room to see a great under-the-radar local band.

A Shock to the System

No matter the act, part of booking these shows is running sound, a job often made more difficult by Tea Bazaar's electrical circuits and small space. As a musician, you've got to adapt to the room. And the person running sound, you've often got to do battle with an overly-loud amplifer (or three).

"Oh god," Brennan Gilmore[†] groan-laughs when asked about the Tea Bazaar. "I played probably my worst, my most unfortunate, evening there," says the bluegrass musician who played punk rock in high school (mohawk and all) and still has a soft spot for loud electric guitar.

BRENNAN GILMORE – Longtime local musician (Walker's Run, Wild Common, etc.) who's also a stellar astrophotographer and advocate for clean energy.

Back in December 2007, Gilmore saw local singer-songwriter Keith Morris (known to at least one fellow musician as Charlottesville "rockin' protest grouch in chief") release his album Songs from Candyapolis at the Gravity Lounge (now The Southern Café & Music Hall).[*] "It's a genius record. I really liked it," says Gilmore, noting that a slew of local artists, including Tea Bazaar regular Devon Sproule, play on it. "It's a very Charlottesville sort of indie lineup." After the show, Gilmore told Morris how much he loved the record and offered to play guitar or mandolin with the band if they needed it for a show. Morris told Gilmore about an upcoming Tea Bazaar set, and so Gilmore learned the songs and a few weeks later, lugged his gear along the Downtown Mall and up the stairs.

His only guitar amp at the time was a Fender Twin Reverb, known among musicians for having, as Gilmore puts it, "incredibly great sound and weighing four tons. They also sound great when you crank them. But if you crank them, they also sound like a supersonic jet."

The amp was maybe too much wattage for the size of the tea house room, but it was the only one Gilmore had. When the band started to play, the amp started making noise "like an asteroid hit the upper atmosphere," says Gilmore, cracking up as he tells the story. "Screeching and rumbling, everybody in the venue is going deaf and I can't make it stop. […] Keith's

---

* Yep, The Southern features in a future issue, too.

got these brilliantly cultivated lyrics and these delicate orchestrations of the band, and my amp is sounding as if two tractor trailers had collided in the middle of the Tea Bazaar. I couldn't do anything about it. I didn't have another amp. I grabbed a mandolin and started playing mandolin, but I didn't have a monitor, and it was really fuckin' loud, and Paul Curreri [Sproule's husband] was out in the audience like, 'turn it down! Turn it down!'

SUREFIRE SIGNS OF A GOOD TEA BAZAAR SHOW INCLUDE, BUT ARE NOT LIMITED TO:

- Rattling a decorative teapot off the high shelves near the stage
- People handing over a $20 bill for a $7 cover and telling the door person to keep the change;
- Expression of thanks and gratitude
- Blown minds
- Making friends and bandmates
- Making it through a set without shorting the electricity, which has been known to zap out fifteen seconds into a band's set, requiring a rearranging of plugs and wires

"I played mandolin on one of Keith's later records, but I never got a call to play live again, with Keith or with anyone else on that stage, because I fuckin' stank up the Tea Bazaar so bad! To my credit, it had nothing to do with my playing and everything to do with my inability to have an actually reasonable road setup for my amp." He's played the room since, but every time he walks through the door, he shudders a little.

"Oh god, it was awful," he says, still laughing. "I hear that sound in my nightmares."

Unforgettable, just like the best Tea Bazaar shows.

A Home for Hip-Hop

Even people with their finger on the pulse of the local scene can overlook what's happening right under their noses.

Dunckel booked as much "weird shit" as she could get, including noise and metal. But it wasn't until Phil Green, a former Tea Bazaar employee who also raps under the moniker "dogfuck," badgered Dunckel that the tea house booked hip-hop.

Green booked the acts, Dunckel ran the show. "I was fucking blown out of the water," says Dunckel. The emcees were excited to have the stage, because, at the time, there weren't many spots in town for the genre. The Bridge Progressive Arts Initiative hosted rap shows, but they had to compete with other programming.* And, by this point Outback Lodge,† Random Row,† and Tokyo Rose were all gone.

During that hip-hop show, Dunckel realized Tea Bazaar wasn't her space — it was a community space, and she needed, wanted, input on booking a wider variety of bills.

A local hip-hop collective, Spititout Inc., started hosting occasional showcases at Eunoia, a Christian, creativity-focused club at UVA, in 2013. Once the group moved its Rugged Arts shows to Tea Bazaar, they became more frequent, hosting local artists and groups plus one out-of-town act roughly once a month.

> **THE OUTBACK LOUNGE –**
> Terry Martin opened the Outback Lodge in 1992 at 917 Preston Avenue, and it hosted everything from hip-hop to street punk and even goth night for a while. It closed in 2010.

"For hip-hop, it's been a real struggle," says rapper Keese Allen, who has lived in Charlottesville his entire life. "Growing up, I would see performances from older rappers and stuff like that, but it was only at certain venues [like Random Row]. It was never all-around town. You couldn't just go downtown and catch a hip-hop show."

> **RANDOM ROW –**
> Random Row Books was a bookshop that also held rock, folk, hip-hop, and art shows, in addition to its literary offerings. The building was demolished to build a hotel. More on page 51.

Before The Annex opened in 2012, Tea Bazaar was pretty much the only downtown space that regularly welcomed hip-hop.

---

*   More on The Bridge PAI also coming in a future issue.

Keese Allen, lifelong Charlottesville resident, longtime rec center employee, and rapper with a positive message.

It hasn't always been easy at Tea Bazaar either, says Remy St. Clair, a local rapper who co-founded and hosts the Rugged Arts series. Artists can build good relationships with one booker, but when that person leaves and another comes in, the artists sometimes must start all over again.

Still, Tea Bazaar "is home," says St. Clair. "I love walking up the steps and seeing that tree. It lets me know that something real is about to happen. Something far out of the norm is to be expected, and it just feels so good. The energy in that place feels so good. It's one of those type of venues where, even if you don't go in there for a hip-hop show, you're going to meet somebody that's very interesting that you're going to be able to click and link with. And chances are, they're not going to be a person, or a vibration, that's in your circle. There's a mix-and-mingle factor."

Keese Allen performs at a Rugged Arts show at Tea Bazaar.
Courtesy of Keese Allen.

"When you walk into Tea Bazaar, there's a guarantee you're going to meet someone who's going to change your perspective, in some way, shape, fashion, or form. Out of all the other venues in the city, you're [...] going to ride on a different vibe when you go into Tea Bazaar," St. Clair adds.

Rugged Arts showcases at Tea Bazaar have given younger rappers like Keese and Malcolm "Waasi" Wills a platform, which is crucial to the health and vibrancy of the genre in a town that's been pretty unwelcoming to hip-hop. For decades, venue owners and managers have used the "it won't draw a crowd" excuse, which rings hollow when hip-hop has been the most popular, best-selling music genre in the United States since 2018, according to the Nielson Soundscan year-end industry report, as cited by *Billboard*. In 2008, a shooting occurred in the parking lot of the Outback Lodge the same night the venue hosted a hip-hop show. Artists maintain that the shooting had nothing to do with the music or with the show, but the incident gave venue owners and managers yet another excuse to deny rappers and DJs a spot on their stages while also skirting the real reason: racism.

Malcolm "Waasi" Wills, a local rapper who has performed in town since he was a teen.

More people should take a moment to listen to the lyrical content of local rappers' music instead of immediately stereotyping and dismissing it, says Wills, another young rapper born and bred in the Charlottesville area. If they did, they'd "understand that it's actually quite positive and uplifting," for the most part, and that's well-suited to Tea Bazaar's overall vibe.

It's why Wills held a release party for his *Betterdaze* EP in January 2018 at the tea house. He packed the place and got a rush from seeing so many people in the room to celebrate and listen with him just as he'd done for other local artists in the same room.

Allen gets a similar feeling when performing in that room. "When you're up there in the Tea Bazaar, you feel like nothing else matters when you're on that stage. You've got the lights and everything. It's a nice, positive venue. I love it. When it's packed in, the vibe is so great because you see people just really tuning in to what you're doing."

Allen remembers a hip-hop acapella show at Tea Bazaar, where the coziness and familiarity of the venue was crucial to the comfort of the performers and the audience during such an unvarnished, intimate performance. "When people see you perform and hear your lyrics, they pay attention. But when there's no beat and it's just your lyrics and the audience, it's a deeper connection, because they actually hear every word you're saying."

Rappers are "fighting for what they believe in, fighting to fully express themselves every time they put pen to pad or every time their fingers hit their iPhone or their iPad to write their poetry, their rhymes, make their true artistry. They are building toward their future. And we as a community around them should do everything in our power to lift them up," St. Clair says. "That's why supporting them is so very important. It's about progress."

Yes, bigger corporate venues in town like John Paul Jones Arena, The Jefferson Theater, and the Sprint Pavilion have booked international rap stars like Cardi B., Da Baby, and Jay-Z, but it's important that the city nurture—and make space for—a local hip-hop scene too, says St. Clair. He notes with disappointment in his voice that more people will pay $150 to see an international star than will pay $5 to see a bill of talented local rappers and DJs.

Not everyone dreams of being an industry star, he adds. Not every artist is meant to travel nationally, internationally, sell out shows and sell hit records. "Some people are meant to make sure home's good. And some people are built to go outside of home and leave. When everybody leaves the nest, there's nobody to tend to home. What do you come back to after all those tours and everything are done? It's very important to make sure that all artists are nurtured, no matter where they want to make it in life, or how big they want to go. Everyone's dream is worth support and nourishment."

St. Clair and his Sons of Ichibei[†] partner Cullen "Fellowman" Wade, along with plenty of others, have continued to host Rugged Arts. In 2017, they established the annual weeklong Nine Pillars Hiphop Cultural Fest, which presents not just performances but graffiti exhibits, lyric and beat competitions, and youth showcases as well.

Sons of Ichibei –

Local rap duo whose Facebook page says they are "dedicated to your destruction, decomposition, and subsequent rebirth. Whether it's with rapid-fire flows or conceptual weight, please understand that they will break you."

"Supporting our own is key to our own system. The money and energy that we put into our own comes right back to us," says St. Clair, who dreams of having a dedicated hip-hop space in town so that this particular music and cultural community can do more than a show or two a month, hold beat-making and lyricism classes and workshops for kids, and more. Performing at the Tea Bazaar is "Shangri-La," he says, and the spot has been vital to the life and growth of hip-hop in Charlottesville.

But still, "independence is very important," says St. Clair, echoing a spirit that's the bedrock of the Tea Bazaar.

A.D. Carson, a professor of hip-hop at UVA, performs at Tea Bazaar.
Photo by Tristan Williams.

The ebb, the flow

As with every venue everywhere, bills evolve and show frequency ebbs and flows, depending not just on who's booking but on how many and what types of bands are active in town at any given time.

And as is true in every music scene everywhere, the "best era" is the one the person you're talking to was involved in.

"It was *the* place to be around that late aughts, early teens time," says Dave Gibson, who has played in a slew of local bands—with a bunch of people he met at the Tea Bazaar—since moving to town in 2007. When Gibson's band, Borrowed Beams of Light, was active, it regularly shared bills, bandmembers, and fans with other locals like The Invisible Hand and Left & Right.[†]

At the time, "everything was still sort of in [corporate] lockdown" as far as venues went, Gibson says. "It was harder to get your foot in the door, because of the fact that so many things were for, or by [Coran] Capshaw.[†] There just weren't that many venues [for independent music], really."

Dave Gibson, film librarian and musician who has played in a slew of local bands, including Weird Mob, Borrowed Beams of Light, the Hilarious Posters, Personal Bandana, and more.

> **BORROWED BEAMS OF LIGHT -**
>
> A psych rock-power pop band active in Charlottesville in the late 2000s/2010s. They released a couple records with Charlottesville-based label WarHen Records.

> **THE INVISIBLE HAND -**
>
> Charlottesville's weirdo indie-rock darlings of the 2000s/2010s. Plenty of folks thought they'd get a big break, since they were just as good, if not better, than most of the bands Pitchfork touted at the time. Another band, Y'ALL, formed from Invisible Hand's ashes.

> **CORAN CAPSHAW -**
>
> A big-time music industry executive who founded Red Light Management (which owns venues like The Southern Café & Music Hall and The Jefferson Theater) in Charlottesville in 1990. He's also a co-founder of ATO Records and manager for the Dave Matthews Band (which, well, ... you know), Phish and Trey Anastasio, Chris Stapleton, and other nationally-touring acts.

> **LEFT & RIGHT -**
>
> A heavy rock band with punk influence. Left & Right was a local favorite before the band relocated to Philadelphia for a chance at indie rock success. They released a slew of recordings, including two full-lengths on WarHen Records.

It takes a little bit of digging to get to the underground music scenes in town, and those people who get involved in bands and/or booking and attending shows tend to be particularly passionate about these types of music. They're willing to do the work to find their people.

Two years after arriving at UVA, in 2012, Amanda Laskey heard that Reading Rainbow, a band she knew from attending Philadelphia-area house shows as a teen, was playing a local show at the Tea Bazaar. She hadn't heard of the place, and outside of a Left & Right set at Random Row, didn't know that other cool things were even happening in Charlottesville. The show wasn't particularly well-attended, but it showed Laskey that she could get involved with music here without having to pay $45 for an LCD Soundsystem ticket. And heavily involved at that.

Amanda Laskey ran shows at Tea Bazaar for a few years, first as an intern with Holy Smokes Booking and later under her own DIY booking agency, Lap The Miles.

"Charlottesville had interesting things going on, and I wanted to be here, and I wanted to be part of this. A lot of UVA didn't appear to have a punk attitude, and I'd been struggling to find that," she says.

Laskey started booking Tea Bazaar in summer 2013, and her philosophy was that she never wanted to book a band just for the money. "I wanted to bring a diverse group of music that represented stuff I was interested in as a younger person. And also music that had been supported at the Tea Bazaar in the past," including the experimental scene. She also collaborated with Dunckel, who was booking DIY/house show spot Magnolia House at the time (and later took over the tea house for Laskey) to make sure they didn't overlap with shows.* At least once, Magnolia House hosted a show earlier in the evening so that Tea Bazaar could host one late night, and people could go to both if they wanted.

---

*   Oh yes, we'll be tackling Charlottesville's beloved DIY/punk spot Magnolia House in the future, too.

Laskey's dream for all Tea Bazaar shows was to have "a rowdy, sweaty show in a weird venue," ones to rival the Left & Right show she saw at Random Row. That didn't always happen, but sometimes it did, and it was amazing, she says. During Laskey's tenure, local bands like Left & Right and Y'ALL played some of the best-sounding sets and drew crowds that sometimes made the floor feel like an accordion. She loved booking quieter shows, too, particularly ones with Grand Banks[†] on the bill. They would (and still do) play a unique ambient set each time.

"Typically, I'd stayed more in the indie rock and punk [vein], but I definitely cried at a Grand Banks show. Those shows changed my entire perspective on a genre of music I'd never really considered." The ability to book folks like Grand Banks' Magill and Salisbury, who were around for the earliest days of the Tea Bazaar in bands like Bucks and Gallants,[†] meant a lot to Laskey, too.

> GRAND BANKS –
>
> The project of longtime Charlottesville experimental music stalwarts Tyler Magill and Davis Salisbury. Formed in 2000, they're still going 22 years later.

Tea Bazaar has been home to both heart- and ear-wrenching shows ranging from uber loud to makes-you-cry soft. (Left) Grand Banks play an acoustic set with Daniel Bachman, renowned American primitive guitar player. All three live in the Charlottesville area. Photo courtesy of Davis Salisbury. (Right) Richmond-based musician Nate Rappole performs as Gull, simultaneously playing guitar and percussion while singing through a face mask he's fashioned into a microphone. Photo by Taylor C.

Another important Tea Bazaar show in Laskey's eyes came from Mannequin Pussy out of Philadelphia. It was a rainy weeknight, which meant most people in Charlottesville (even the ones who claim to love music) stayed home. The show was sparsely attended, Laskey remembers, but that didn't make a difference. "It was probably one of the first times we'd had a primarily female lineup," she says. Laskey remembers bandmember Marisa Dabice thanking her for running sound, for actually listening to them and adjusting all the levels to get a great mix through the monitors facing the band, and through the speakers for the audience. Dabice also told Laskey that most times, the people running sound for their shows are men who ignore the band, but on the rare occasion that a woman was running the board, she was always attentive.

Laskey has always understood and championed the importance of having women in the DIY scene, but in that moment, she realized that it was important to have women in every corner of music, from shredding on stage to running sound to booking shows, and more. It made her feel good to be a part of that.

Tea Bazaar Today

As its non-corporate, open-minded venue peers have closed, and as the corporate venues have shunned some of the music that Tea Bazaar welcomes, the tea house presses on, more than 20 years after its birth.

"I'm glad it's still around," says Sam Roberts, who's drummed in a bunch of Central Virginia punk bands, including Wild Rose and Fried Egg, and lived at and booked Magnolia House for a few years. "It kind of represents an earlier time of Charlottesville. All kinds of places like that that are still around, [and] I'm glad to have [them]. It seems like there's always more businesses in town, but when a cool place closes, it's probably not going to be replaced by another cool place."

When the COVID-19 pandemic shut down live shows in March 2020, the Tea Bazaar stopped hosting music, and, as of publication time, hasn't had a show since. Rumor says they're unsure if, or when, live music will return.

Fried Egg, featuring Tyler Abernethy on guitar, Sam Roberts on drums, Erik Tsow on vocals, and Sam Richardson on bass. Both Sams played crucial roles in DIY Charlottesville music: Roberts lived at and booked Magnolia House, and Richardson booked Dust Warehouse. Photo by Juliana Caycedo, courtesy of Sam Roberts.

But over two decades isn't so bad for a place with a stage built as an afterthought. A place that some folks didn't think would last very long in this town.

But rapper Keese offers an idea as to why it's survived: "As soon as you walk in that place, there's something that catches you. You just don't want to leave."

Matteus Frankovich at the Tea Bazaar's one-year anniversary party in 2003.

Interlude:

Art from Two Decades of Shows at Tea Bazaar

James Ford, aka DJ Hummingbird Feeder, created all of the flyers in this gallery. He not only designed posters for Tea Bazaar shows, he helped book a few as well. Ford lives in Baltimore now, but when he was in Charlottesville, he DJed at WTJU, wrote a music column for C-VILLE Weekly, and was the driving force behind the Nailgun Media music blog.

ANDREW CEDERMARK
WEIRD MOB
ERIK the RED

Saturday, July 20th $7.00
Twisted Branch Tea Bazaar   9:00pm

DRUNK TIGERS
INVISIBLE HAND
Twisted Branch
Tea Bazaar
Saturday May 11th

70 & 71: Tigers

53) ESCAPE ON VENUS
(Pages No. 39)

35 SALOME The Black Cape

The Crescent and Its Combinations

9:00pm
$7.00

CHRIS CORSANO
GOLDEN GLASSES &
MATT NORTHRUP
DAIS QUEUE
NU DEPTH

Twisted Branch Tea Bazaar

DENSITY CONTROL GUARANTEED

**Monday,
September 10th**

$7.00 9:00pm   651-18   1242

CHAIN & the GANG
(Ian Svenonius, K Records)

the HA - RANG !!
SHARK WEEK

Thursday, August 15th   **$7.00**
Twisted Branch Tea Bazaar   **9:00 pm**

Daniel Bachman
Dais Queue

Friday April 26th
Twisted Branch
Tea Bazaar

ISBN 0-486-23785-0

9 780486 237855

$5.00   9:00 PM

Old Paw   34

Tapping up and down the road in a frenzy, and groping
and calling for his comrades.

HALLOWEEN DANCE PARTY

Twisted Branch Tea Bazaar $0.00–$5.00

Thursday, October 31st   9:00 PM – 1:00 AM

DEATH LIVES!

GLENN JONES
GRAND BANKS

Twisted Branch Tea Bazaar
Saturday, July 6
9:00 $7.00

HOLY SMOKES BOOKING PRESENTS

DUMP

(JAMES McNEW of YO LA TENGO)

SLOPPY HEADS

GIRL CHOIR

TWISTED BRANCH TEA BAZAAR

SATURDAY, AUGUST 13TH   9PM

$8   get tickets at www.holysmokesbooking.com

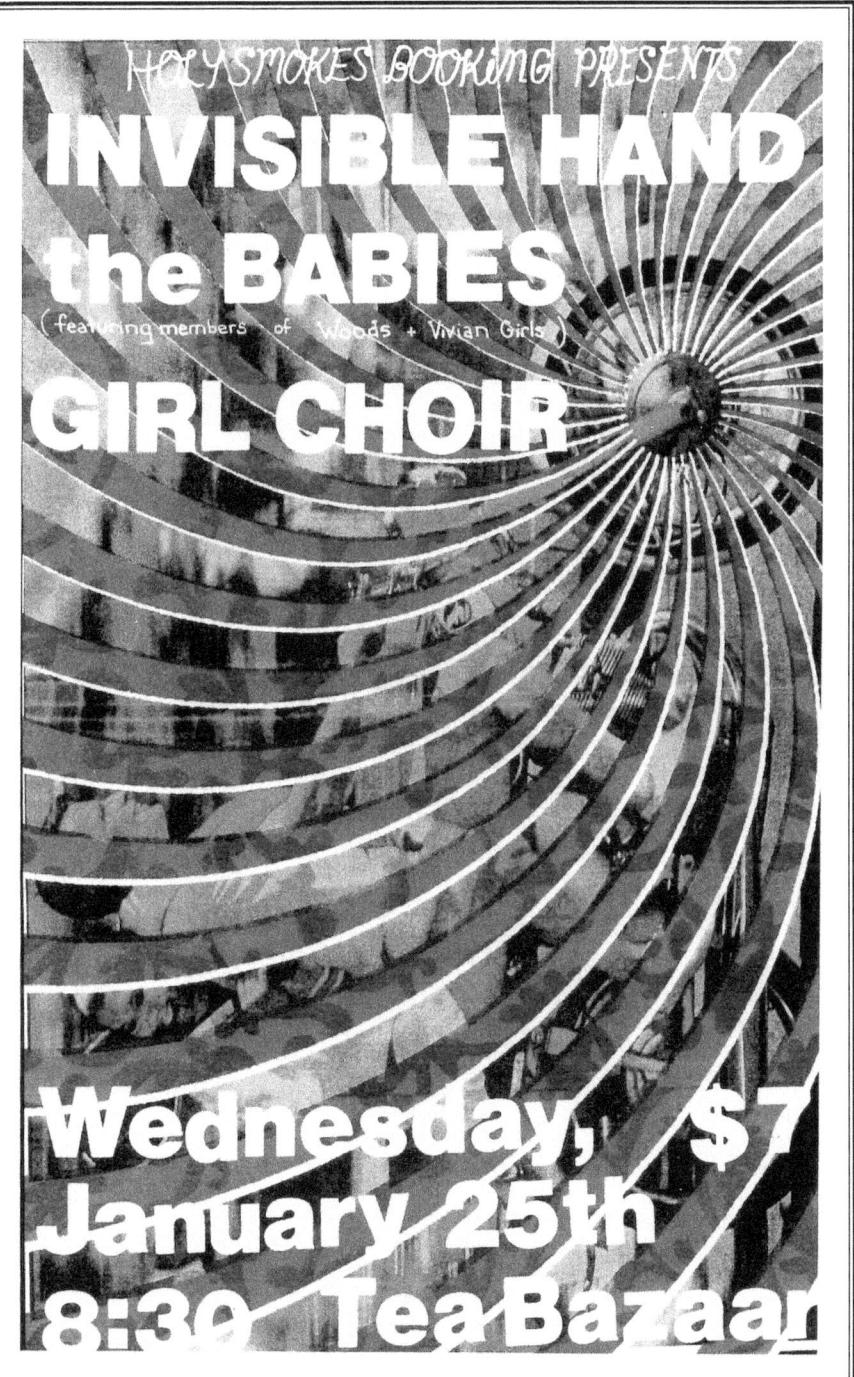

HOLYSMOKES BOOKING PRESENTS

INVISIBLE HAND

the BABIES
(featuring members of Woods + Vivian Girls)

GIRL CHOIR

**Wednesday, $7
January 25th
8:30 Tea Bazaar**

DANIEL BACHMAN
NATHAN BOWLES
DAIS QUEUE

Twisted Branch Tea Bazaar   9:00 PM
Friday, November 22ND $7.00

GRAND BANKS
ALAMEDA
BEN SERETAN

Twisted Branch Tea Bazaar $7.00
Friday, October 18th   9:00pm

Eternal Summers
Andrew Cedermark
Greenland
Family Trees

Tea Bazaar   Friday June 18th

WOODS
PARQUET COURTS
LEFT & RIGHT

Tuesday, July 23rd
Twisted Branch Tea Bazaar

stereo $8.00/8:30...

45

WTJU 91.1 fm
2013 Rock
Marathon
Dance Party

live music by Savoir Adore
DJs from WTJU
9pm - 12:00am
sliding scale $5-$20
all proceeds go towards the
WTJU 2013 spring fundraiser

Friday, April 5.

Twisted Branch   Tea Bazaar

the LOVE LANGUAGE
ETERNAL SUMMERS
the MINGSLEYS

Twisted Branch Tea Bazaar
Sat, Aug 3rd
$8.00 9:00pm

MOD SOUL Dance Party

DJ Tanner
Kimmy Gibbler
from WTJU

Hummingbird Feeder
DJ Helvidious
from WTJU

Tea Bazaar Sat Dec 6 9pm

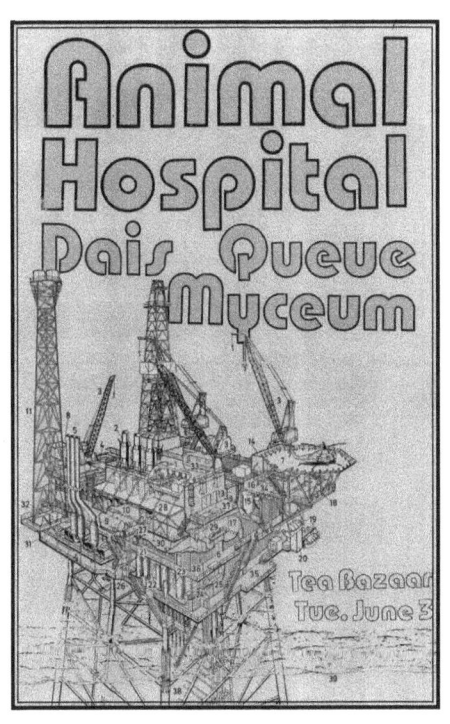

WTJU

a fundraiser dance party
Saturday, October 31st

$5 cover charge
wear a costume!

wtjurock.blogspot.com   DJ Hummingbird Feeder   Ming the Mer

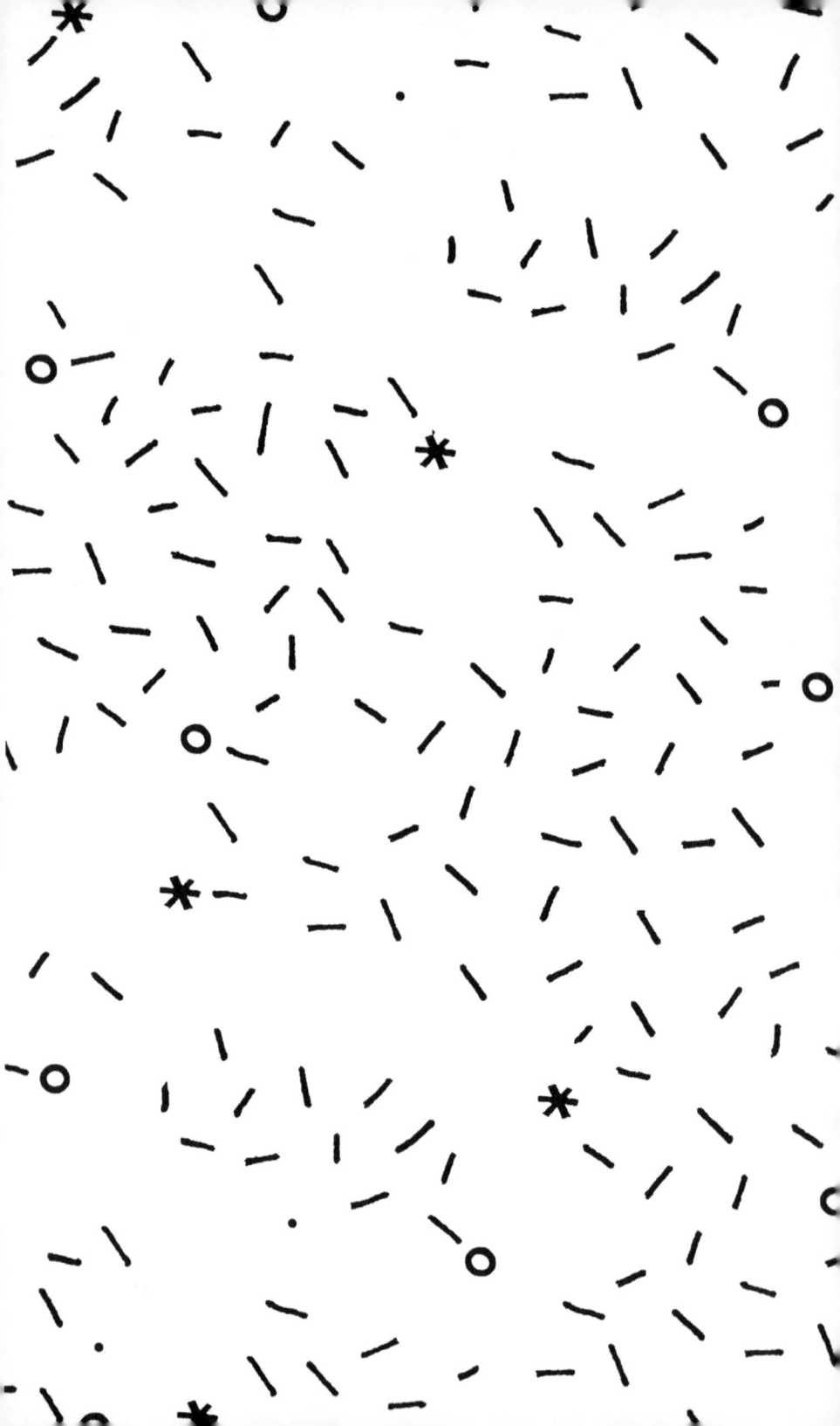

Bonus Tracks

Continuing the Legacy of Random Row and Tokyo Rose

The web of Charlottesville music is always being undone and re-spun, with places closing and opening, or starting and stopping support for local music. Scenes evolve as venues change hands, booking agents leave town, bands break up, venues close, and new groups arise to fill voids left by former pillars of the music community.

Random Row Books and Tokyo Rose are two venues whose musical legacies are entwined with that of Tea Bazaar, and who have helped cultivate some of the very same scenes that ended up—and further evolved—downtown at the tea house. With rich histories in their own right, we could have easily written entire zines on either location, especially Tokyo Rose, which held influence on a national level.

Both Random Row and Tokyo Rose have been closed as music venues for years. With the future of live music at Tea Bazaar uncertain, it remains to be seen what venues and groups will take up and adapt their legacy for the 2020s and beyond.

Rock Bookshop: Random Row

Random Row Books, located at 315 W. Main Street, opened in fall 2009 at the corner of West Main and Ridge/McIntire, and closed in June 2013, much to the underground arts scene's dismay. It held rock, folk, hip-hop, and art shows in addition to its literary offerings. In true Charlottesville fashion, the building was demolished to build a hotel.

Photo courtesy of Maureen Brondyke.

Told by rapper, local high school teacher, and WTJU DJ Cullen Wade, who goes by Fellowman when he raps and Mr. Owl when he hosts radio shows. The following is his recounting of what the bookstore and venue has meant to him and the local music community. He revived the "Cadmium" metal show on WTJU in 2022.

I owe my entire existence as a musical and performing artistic entity in the city of Charlottesville to Random Row. I came here in the summer of 2011, fresh from my Peace Corps service and intending to attend grad school at UVA for teaching. (I dropped out, but ended up being a teacher anyway.) I saw this flyer somewhere on the UVA Corner for an open mic: *Just Lyricz,* the first and third Wednesday of every month, at Random Row.

It was predominately a bookstore, and had caught my eye on my very first day in Charlottesville. Riding by on my bike, it was hard not to pull a cartoonish brake-screech stop and pull over; it was a really eye-catching and funky-looking place.

The building had a very warehouse feel: unpainted, raw concrete walls, high ceiling, and shelves so tall you had no idea how to get something off the top. You'd walk in through a little entryway with bookshelves on either side, before the room opened up into a larger space. The walls were lined with art: I remember one painting in particular, a Japanese samurai or shogun. The right side, lined with the aforementioned very tall bookshelves, held most of the inventory. And on the left side, a big, open space with a stage.

There used to be several of these kinds of places in Charlottesville. Not really anymore.

All this to say, I languished, upset, when I was stuck in class on that Wednesday, missing the open mic, this incredibly cool venue, and an entry ticket to the music scene.

Fast-forward to February 2012, at a Black History Month event at UVA put on by DJ Double A1K (Anthony Amos) and organized by the same people who did the Just Lyricz open mic. It's where I met Anthony, Tracy Saxon (aka R.U.N.T. 215th), and Harli Saxon. It's also the first time I performed.

After, they told me, "You need to come and be part of this!" So, next semester, I deliberately arranged my class schedule so I could go to Just Lyricz at Random Row. And that was the start of everything.

I saw some amazing, amazing performers there. Saw some great shows, some features that were brought from the Richmond slam scene; it was where I met G Yamazawa [based in Durham], Matthew Cuban [based in L.A.], and of course, it was where I met Remy St. Clair.

I was in a group, Spititout, Inc., with Tracy and Remy for several years after that. I'm still in a group with Remy, called Sons of Ichibei. We started the Rugged Arts hip-hop showcase together. We later started the Nine Pillars Hip Hop Cultural Fest together, in 2017.

After Anthony moved to the D.C. area, we continued the open mic, which by that time had changed its name to Verbs & Vibes, until 2015. It moved to Para Coffee on the Corner for a while, before it was Grit, and then to The Bridge PAI. Random Row was where I met a lot of people that have been involved in Nine Pillars since then. I owe all of it to those connections I made at Random Row and Just Lyricz, to the magnetism that drew a certain kind of person in.

Looking back at that whole Just Lyricz/Verbs & Vibes crew, it was the perfect confluence of the right people, the right mission, and the right space, all at the right time.

And then things change, people and times move on. Bookstores get bought out and torn down and turned into hotels. Life is a constant search for what comes after: the next right place, the next group of passionate, like-minded people. To be in the room at the right time for the next iteration of something special.

(Left to Right) Jamal Millner, Gina Sobel, Daniel Richardson, Cathy Monnes, and Chris Dammann play freaky free jazz at an ELECTRIC Love and Eggrolls show at Random Row in June 2013. Photo by Martin Phillips, courtesy of Gina Sobel. (Fun fact: Daniel, Jack, and Sam Richardson, all of whom appear in photos in this issue, are brothers.)

Sushi Goth: Tokyo Rose

Atsushi Miura opened Tokyo Rose at 2171 Ivy Road in the 1980s. Throughout the 1980s, 1990s, and early 2000s, the unfinished basement of this legitimate sushi restaurant operated as a music club and welcoming home for a (literally) underground punk, rock, goth, and indie scene. Miuri sold the business in 2004, and despite occasional shows over the next couple of years, music at Tokyo Rose had been brought to an end by 2007. The restaurant itself closed in 2022. The building is now home to El Tio Restaurant y Tienda, an admittedly delicious Salvadoran restaurant and store.

A Tokyo Rose show. Photo by Danny Shea.

Music fanatic and sushi chef Atsushi Miura welcomed music into the basement of his restaurant at 2271 Ivy Rd. throughout the 1990s and early 2000s, and it had a massive effect on the local rock scene.

Darius Van Arman, who also founded the Jagjaguwar record label,[†] booked shows there for a time, often styling a season's show calendar like a menu. Tokyo Rose was a home for local and touring acts, particularly edgier bands playing weird indie rock, punk, hardcore, metal, garage, and rock' n' roll. Somehow, international indie rock royalty like Cat Power, Will Oldham (who has Charlottesville connections), SMOG, Neutral Milk Hotel, and riot grrrl's Sleater-Kinney made Tokyo Rose a stop on their national tours.

> Van Arman founded Jagjaguwar in Charlottesville in 1996 before relocating to Bloomington, Illinois, in 1999. The label has released hundreds of albums from indie rock superstars like Bon Iver and Angel Olsen, but its first release was Bombay Aloo from The Curious Digit, a Charlottesville band that played poetic, herky-jerky avant-pop. Other early releases came from local artists, too, like Sarah White and Manishevitz.

The April 1996 Sleater-Kinney/Curious Digit show at Tokyo Rose was one of the best that Rob Sheffield, longtime contributing editor to Rolling Stone Magazine and former Charlottesville resident and WTJU DJ, has seen. He told C-VILLE Weekly in 2020 that it was "one of the peak music moments" of his life. It was right after Sleater-Kinney's *Call the Doctor* album came out, and it was a benefit for the Charlottesville nonprofit Sexual Assault Resource Agency. Sheffield's friend Jeanine, who emceed the show and had ties to both SARA and WTJU, tossed her bra up on the stage and it caught on Sleater-Kinney singer Corin Tucker's mic. Tucker kept it there all night.

Miura and Van Arman paid bands relatively well and attracted a dedicated crowd, which made the place all that more attractive on the Boston to Atlanta tour run.

"That era of music in town was pretty amazing," says Tyler Magill.

It was a special place, too, says Magill, in the way that people mingled and came up with cool, weird ideas. "People talked, people became friends with each other. They would talk about these incredibly goofy fucking ideas they had, and people would be like, 'yeah, okay, I'm not doing anything Thursday. Let's dress up as bears.'"

Miura—who himself was known to do an excellent cover of Roy Orbison's "Crying"—sold the spot in 2004, leaving a gaping hole in the rock music scene that other venues had to work to make up. Unfortunately, no venue's come close to being that cool and influential on a national level since (except, maybe, Magnolia House).

The restaurant itself closed in 2022.

A Hillbilly Werewolf show at Tokyo Rose. Hillbilly Werewolf played trashy garage-punk, though some might say there was some rockabilly in there, too. Photo by Danny Shea

Lead singer Scotty Mominee of Hillbilly Werewolf, a garage-punk band that often played Tokyo Rose, in his show attire. Scottie passed one of his guitars down to Fried Egg's Richardson.

The Cherry Valence at Tokyo Rose

Told by Jordan Perry, known in some circles for his American Primitive-style guitar playing. In other circles, he's one of the singers and guitar players for Charlottesville twee-boogie band New Boss. In still other circles, he was in a bunch of hardcore bands in Harrisonburg (where he lived in longstanding DIY punk spot Crayola House) and Philadelphia. He was attending and playing shows at Tokyo Rose before he moved to town.

"That's where I got my head broken open on stage. I played a show with my band from Harrisonburg — we were opening for the Cherry Valence. My guitar fell off, and the bass player didn't see me and just swung around really hard and clocked me in the skull with the headstock of his bass. But anyway, I just started gushing blood down my face, and the singer was kind of into shocking people, and he wiped my blood off my head and smeared it on his face. It was pretty fucking crazy. And I had kind of a crush on the guitar player from Cherry Valence…. And she put a t-shirt on my head. I was so excited that I was like, 'oh my gosh, hi. You're really cool, and you're putting a t-shirt on my bloody head.'"

Synthetic Division at Tokyo Rose

Told by Shawn Decker, who performed as Synthetic Division for more than 20 years, making electronic music that aimed to move both the heart and the feet. He discontinued the project in 2022 after playing a Stranger Things-*themed show at The Jefferson Theater. Decker and his wife, Gwenn Barringer, are world-renowned for their HIV/AIDS education and advocacy efforts. Here, he talks about how Tokyo Rose—and the people he met there—changed his life.*

When I first moved to Charlottesville, I didn't know what the music scene was like. The only music I knew from Charlottesville was Dave Matthews Band, so wasn't quite sure how I'd fit in with my electronic music. A writer at C-VILLE Weekly who was interviewing me and Gwenn about our HIV work said, "Oh, you like all this music? You like Depeche Mode and The Cure? You have to meet this guy Gopal Metro."

I went to Cosmic Coyote on The Corner (a little store that sold some various eccentric items, like hair dye and all that stuff) met Gopal, and gave him my Synthetic Division CD. He popped it in, listened to it, and Gopal was like, "Yeah, we got a spot [at The Dawning] in six weeks. Be ready."

Shawn Decker, formerly of goth-y synth band Synthetic Division, a writer for POZ Magazine, and author of My Pet Virus: The True Story of a Rebel Without a Cure.

So, I booked my first show as Synthetic Division right after I moved to Charlottesville, in 1999. It was right after Gwenn and I got together, and I was pretty sick at the time, too, but I was so excited to play. Gwenn would carry most of my equipment down the steps of Tokyo Rose.

The Dawning nights, usually Saturday nights, were pretty awesome. The basement of Tokyo Rose definitely had its vibe, with people upstairs eating sushi and out drinking, and then they had the bar downstairs [with music]. I had friends who worked the bar. It was great.

By April 2001, I was playing The Dawning—goth nights at Tokyo Rose—semi-regularly, and the Dave Matthews Band was coming back to play a Charlottesville show after achieving worldwide fame. Gwenn and I had been traveling around, educating together as a couple; I'd started HIV meds, my health had come back. I was healthy enough to travel and carry my own equipment down the Tokyo Rose steps by the time that show happened. We'd been speaking to college students around the country, and when they heard we were from Charlottesville, the history people would be, "Oh, Thomas Jefferson." Everybody else was like, "Oh, Dave Matthews Band is from there!"

So, Dave Matthews Band was getting ready to play its big Charlottesville show at Scott Stadium. It was mid-week, a Wednesday or something. I got this idea that a [faux] "battle of the bands" would be hilarious, and I found out there wasn't a band booked to play Tokyo Rose [that night], even though they didn't really take many nights off. I contacted Gopal and pitched him the idea, and he thought it was hilarious. I made up that flyer and put it up … it was funny.

I think there were maybe 40 people at The Dawning that night, which, in the basement of Tokyo Rose, anything above 20 felt like a good night! Most times it was more than that, but it was cool that people came out; they didn't know anybody was playing that night. It was very last-minute, but that's what makes it cool.

You had this big concert where [almost] everybody in town was jockeying for tickets....But we had this little last-minute show at Tokyo Rose, in our own little corner of the Charlottesville music scene. I just remember thinking the idea was funny, being excited that nobody was playing, that I could make up this flyer and do this whole thing acknowledging what was consuming a lot of energy in this town, but we're going to battle against that.

SATURDAY APRIL 21st 2001
BATTLE of the BANDS
FINALLY, ONCE AND FOR ALL, WE'LL FIND OUT WHO C'VILLE'S BEST TRULY IS!

VS.

SYNTHETIC DIVISION live at Tokyo Rose	DAVE MATTHEWS BAND live at Scotts Stadium
OVER 20 ALBUMS SOLD	OVER 20 MILLION ALBUMS SOLD
STRUGGLING WITH AIDS	STRUGGLING WITH BOTTLE
TICKETS ARE 5.00	TICKETS ARE 50.00

WHO WILL OUTDRAW WHO?
IT'S UP TO YOU!

Show flyer by Shawn Decker.

Midway through my set, I probably claimed victory or something obnoxious, said something like, "thanks for coming out tonight to rage against the fuckin' machine!" I kind of stumbled over it, it was kind of awkward. But it was fun, a really chill night. Tokyo Rose always had a supportive, built-in crowd. It was what I was always hoping for when I was a teenager and just working my stuff: to play a show, to be part of a music scene.

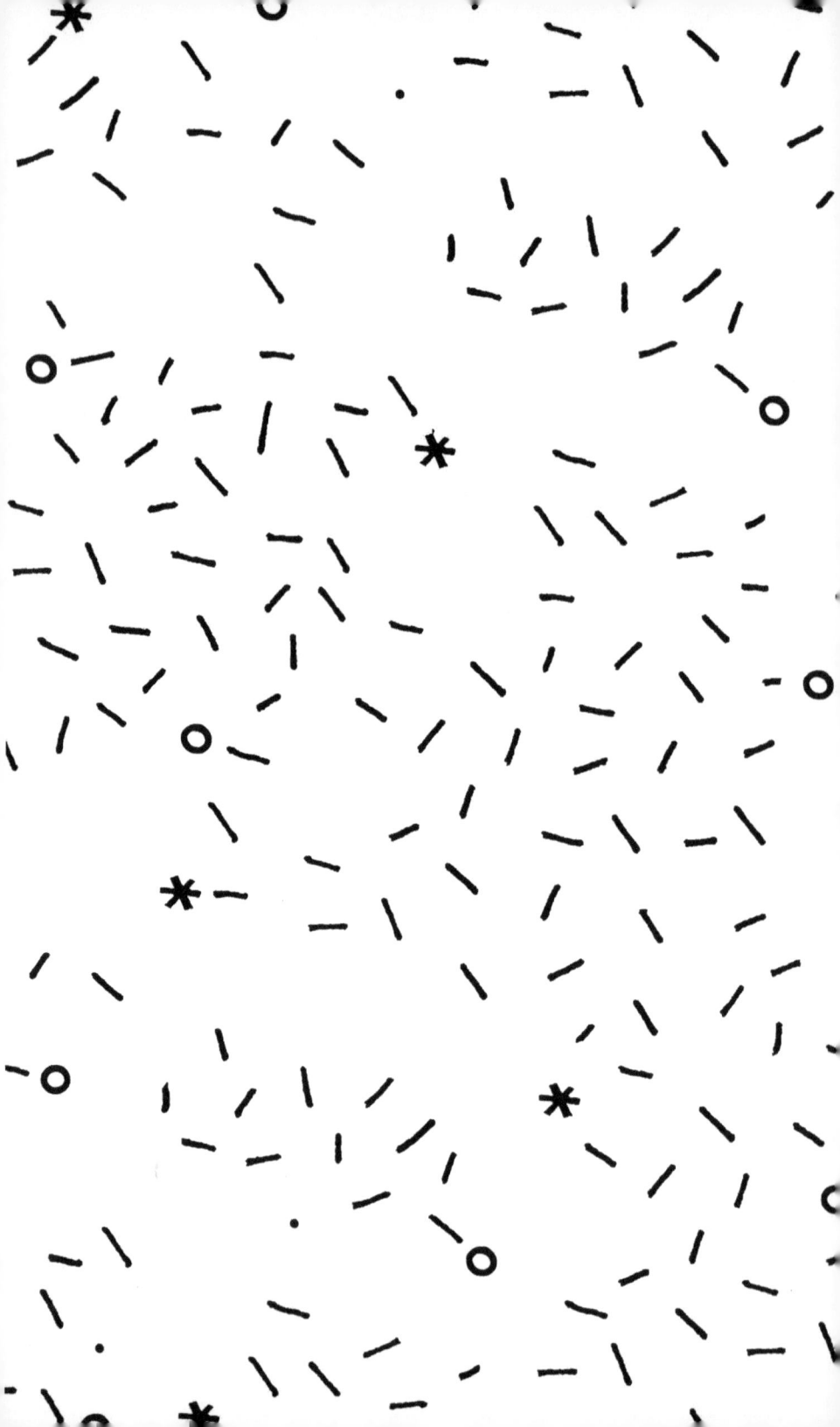

Acknowledgements

For their contributions to the Charlottesville music scene and to the author during the researching, interviewing, and writing process for this book *about* that scene, a very loud and warm thanks to:

Keese Allen

Matthew Burtner

A.D. Carson

Richelle Claiborne

Kittie Cooper

Shawn Decker

Annie Dunckel

Jeyon Falsini

Mattheus Frankovich

Dave Gibson

Brennan Gilmore

Alan Goffinski

Dhara Goradia

Lester Jackson

Amanda Laskey

Leslie Morgan Lowry

Tyler Magill

Cathy Monnes

Jordan Perry

Jay Pun

Renee Reighart

Sam Roberts

Davis Salisbury

Danny Shea

Matthew Simon

Steve Snider

Gina Sobel

Devon Sproule

Remy St. Clair

Travis Thatcher

Cullen Wade

Sarah White

Malcolm Wills

Special Thanks

This project would not have been possible without the generous funding of WTJU, the University of Virginia, and Virginia Humanities. Our especial gratitude to WTJU Radio, the UVA Vice Provost for the Arts, UVA Arts Council, and Virginia Humanities.

This project is also indebted to the work of two illustrious artists. The portraits that appear throughout are the work of Sarah Everton, whose work can be found at sarah-everton.com. The cover art was created by printer, illustrator, and Charlottesville musician Thomas Dean. Below is an image of one of many of Thomas's bands, Order—previously Order of the Dying Orchid—performing at Tea Bazaar.

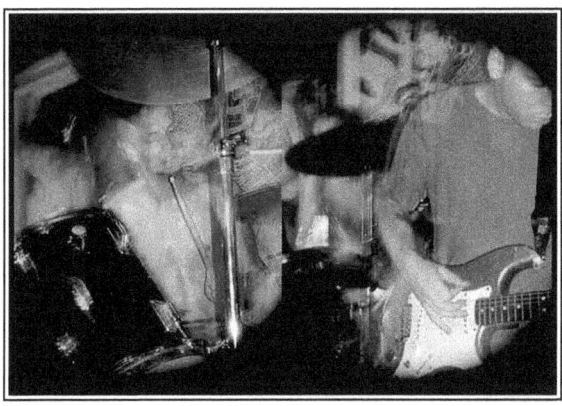

About the Author

Erin O'Hare is a local journalist, musician, and DJ, co-hosting *Ye Olde Tuesday Afternoon Rocke Show* and *Black Circle Revolution* on WTJU 91.1 FM/wtju.net. She also books music at Visible Records, a community art studio and gallery space that contains an antifascist book shop. For at least 40 hours each week, she is the neighborhoods reporter for the community-focused Charlottesville Tomorrow, where she writes in-depth stories mostly about housing, specifically the ongoing housing crisis.

Erin had wanted to write a book since she started reading them when she was four. She did, and it was harder and a lot less fun than she thought. Now that book manuscript is this zine series, which was also harder, but a lot more fun, than she thought.

She lives in so-called Charlottesville, on unceded Monacan and Manahoac lands, with her partner (who she met while writing this very series), their two cats, and their out of control record collection.